Wayne's World
of Motivational Words

DWAYNE LAKE

Order this book online at www.trafford.com
or email orders@trafford.com

Most Trafford titles are also available at major online book retailers.

Print information available on the last page.

ISBN: 978-1-4907-7311-7 (sc)
ISBN: 978-1-4907-7310-0 (e)

Trafford rev. 05/20/2016

Trafford www.trafford.com
PUBLISHING
North America & international
toll-free: 1 888 232 4444 (USA & Canada)
fax: 812 355 4082

CONTENTS

Acknowledgements

First giving honor and thanks to my maker and creator my Lord God, my savior Jesus Christ, the Holy Spirit, My Parents Claude and Eddie Mae Lake, My brother Claude Stephun Lake Jr. My Sister Patricia Foster, My Nephew Stephun Lake, My Nephew Doug Foster, My Nieces, Nikki Holmes, Meka Foster, My Uncles, Lonnie and Frank Loyd, My Aunt, Grace Hunter, My Aunt's Altha Bradly, Audrey Henderson, Laura, Mae, Dean, Doris, Gwen, My Uncles Willie Cox, Archie Davis, Oga, W.L.(Blue) Kent, to all my Cousin and Friends, my brothers from another mother, Son Of Zion Pastor Vidal Cargo, Freddie Williams, Dexter Brady, Cousins Minister Nathan Henderson, Thanks for vocal training, Josph Murphy for managing us, Founder Bishop Charles and Maxine Stimage, Pastor Willie Marrow, Zion Grove Baptist Church, Will Do Citizen Cadet Corp Drill Team, for teaching me discipline, endurance patients, respect, maturity, Hirsch Metropolitan Class of "89" All my Huskies, Securitas, inc. 15 years of service, Antoinette Johnson (toni)helping with data processing, people that inspired me, The Winans, Commissioned Fred Hammond, thank for meeting me and my brother back stage. The Kings of Comedy, Martin, Mike Epps, Kevin Hart, Bruce Bruce, Rickey Smiley, The Wayans, Rakim, KRS1, Nas, LL Cool J, Run DMC, X Clan, Public Enemy, Method Man, Michael Jordan, Michael Jackson, Martin Luther King, President Obama, to my god mother Mamie Smith Oaks after Aunts and Uncles

AMERICA

America have you heard
It's a brand new day and I bring the word
I don't need you conviction or life reality
I just want a word from God in actuality
He told me just to live right to always do his will
Always honor parents, never kill or steal
Do the things I know right stay away from wrong
If I keep his will, my days on earth be long
I don't have to worry, never have to fret
Every one of my needs, yes my Lord has met
You can't make me wonder, you can't make cry
God is but the only I'll lay my life and die
You can pray to Buda, I hope to you he bless
I only know one God, Alpha and omega, no contest
The president can't lead us to have peace on earth
For years they have shown us what they really worth
So you trust your Alderman or Secretary of state
Most of them about the money lie plus hate
Debate never waits from the house verse the congress
America now broke by the drama to the mess
God he the only answer, my father is the key
He can save the world, both you and me

Written
By
Dwayne Lake

I TRY

I try no lie better to laugh than cry,
I try to love, than make war
God has more for us in store
I try to appreciate not hate
All the drama and debate can wait
I try to give more than receive
In my God I do believe
I try to be all can be
I'm in the Lord's army
I try to teach maybe preach
I pray the youth, I can reach
I try to answer when I'm called
Let's get back up, when we fall
I try to open up my heart
Give this world a little part
I try to be a better man
To follow my Lord's master plan
I try to sing, I've got to pray
Ask my God, to take me his way

Written by
Dwayne Lake

YOU CHOOSE

Get yo butt up out yo seat
Go to them streets and move yo feet
You can get out to get a job
Or stay home and be a slob
You can enroll in a school
Or play in the hood like a fool
You can stand in front of the store
Then beg for a little more
Be out on the corner selling drugs
Or do it legal selling pillows and rugs
You can wait in line all day for link
Or use yo brain, yo mind to think
Of a plan to earn some legit money
This is the land of milk and honey
Be a stripper or palyboy bunny
Or sell lemonade when days are sunny
Sell water, chips or snowballs
Or climb over somebody's property wall
you can be all that you can be
Join airforce, MArines, Army or Navy
Do crime Go straight to jail
Keep the sin Then fall to hell
While you do your stop I rather spend my life in Heaven.

I SEE YOU

Get your money, Make your Loot
Wear your gators, Armani Suits
Claim your Man, He is your boo
Wear your hells, them Jimmy Choo
Drive your Beamer, Benz and Lex
You get Real Estate collect your checks
Receive your lady, she is your prize
Make other Brothers Realize, open eyes
Be a King this is your earth
Show the World, What your Worth
You're a Queen, You got your Ring
You can accomplish anything
Get your House, Make it a home
Let them Know this is you throne
You can Rise above any mess
They be impressed how fresh you dressed
Remove yourself from all the drama
Let them save that for their Momma
I like the way you command, demand respected
Then you always protect your neck
You do your thing, you make me proud
The way you stand out in a crowd

Written by
Dwayne Lake

JUST DO IT

You don't have to follow
　Know that you can be the Lead
Don't let money or the power
　Give you the need for greed
　　　　　　　　　Be yourself
　　　　　　　　　Like none other be you
　　　　　　　　　Whatever you do
　　　　　　　　　Keep it real be true
You're the worth of the earth
　Prince, Princess, King and Queen
Set your mind to your goal
　You can do anything
　　　　　　　　　The world is yours to have
　　　　　　　　　Just as long as you can plan
　　　　　　　　　You have to make it happen
　　　　　　　　　Be the Women or the Man

　　　　　　　　　　　Written By
　　　　　　　　　　　Dwayne Lake

Dwayne Lake

HEAR MY DEAR

I am here dear to dry your tear
I want to start to mend your broken heart
Always around a while to make you smile
I'll be that coffee in your cup to lift you up
I will dedicated to motivate you
Check to be the knight to protect
Have the plan to be the man
Give you my all we'll have a ball
Laugh and play enjoy everyday
Spend quality time we'll wine and dine
Through any type of weather join closer together
Our funds we'll stack have each other's back
Never attack or over react
Be exact, truthful state the fact
Won't fuss but have plenty of trust
Under the heaven above share our love
Promise to care and always share
Be the king, get you a ring
Put it on your hand then purchase us land
Make you my wife, together forever spend our life

Written By
Dwayne Lake

MY GOD

You are my Lord, King and Savior
Thank you for your life long favor
For watching our back keeping us alive
Whenever there is danger on time you arrive
You're always there to protect our neck
You've always blessed us with a paycheck
Roof over our heads, with cloths on our back
In those streets, kept us from getting jacked
You been there for us many long years
Through heart aches tears and fears
Whenever down your words have uplifted
With life, love, health and wealth you've gifted
Your son walked on water you parted the red sea
I thank you My Lord God, you created me
We look to your signs, miracles and wonders
You pick us up, dust us off, whenever we blinder
Every day I pray, you forgive us for our sin
In you there is no failure you're the beginning and
The end

Written by
Dwayne Lake

MY PEOPLE

My brother from another mother unlike none other
Can we extend to join our hand sit down to mke a plan can
we please come together no matter what the weather get
to know each other better become stronger than leather
unite without a fight get our kids and do what is right
My sister, Mother, Queen
For you I do anything
Can we better relate
Join together, talk, not hate try to better understand
communicate to comprehend form our minds on one
accord put down those guns, shields and swords
Restore the families, break some bread
Let's be mature, Intelligent use our heads.

MAKE DOLLARS

If It dont make dollar it dont make sense
Aint nothing going on but my note and the rest
The money and the power what beings respect
without the money aint a damn thing funny
If you got it then you happy, then yours days are sunny
The root of evil drive some people to bad devidens
are some friends a means to an end
Funds put before God now that's a sin
A no win life situation to have
Some dont have money no time to laugh
So get to the streets better move your feet because you
know your people's got to eat keep a roof over head
plus all bills paid use your muscles just to hustle there's
money to be made money is time and time is money
you must put in work for the milk and honey
Nothing comes easy there's nothing for free
So work hard, money can be plenty for both you and me.

My Chocolate

The darker the chocolate the richer the taste
The flavor smell so good put a smile on my face
Open up your mind so that we can explore
Chocolate can be sweet like an Almond Joy
Hershey my delight so thick likes the mounds
I love them Reese's Pieces, peanut butter by pounds
Your hugs and your kisses' so tender so pure
It makes me feel so better you Milky Way is the cure
Snickers so smooth so silky so sweet
M&M so scrumptious inviting to eat
I nibble on the peanuts I love it a bunch
I try, no lie,to bite it, but I can't help to munch
I fix my lips to taste the Twix
Those chocolate sticks what a wonderful mix
These chocolate covered bars, send me to mars
Make me feel like heaven, between all the stars

Written by
Dwayne Lake

STAY FOCUSED

Keep yo eyes on the prize you mind on yo goal
Strive for yo dream but don't sell yo soul
Believe in yourself or your true religion
Keep yo head on straight then tunnel yo vision
Stay up on them tracks yo money keep stack
Continue piling it, until you reaching the max
We all have to hustle so stay on yo grind
Keep that thing sharp yo third eye, yo mine
Watch out for distractions for they throw you off
Bend but don't break that don't mean you soft
You're more than a number so stand and be counted
Like a statue stand strong, don't be pushed be mounted
If you standing for something don't fall for it all
Live yo life to the fullest plus please has a ball
Wolves in sheep clothing are out there to eat
Be strong as a lion, be the one to defeat

Written by
Dwayne Lake

Haters hate

Those sticks and stones won't hurt my bones
You can talk about me, but stay in your zone
Yeah laugh in my face stab me in my back
Then when I'm around you react with attack
You try to put me down you act like clown
You'll know I mean business if you get off the ground
A face full of envy, I wear Gucci and Guess
I'm just looking by best, I'm dressed to impress
I never look down, on what's on your plate
Why do you have hate, for your time, wont you wait
When I come around, you turn up your noise
Do you have to be mad, cause I wear fresh cloths
Why act stanky like that, do you must be that way
Is this hate just because, a Benz in my drive way
Your time to shine is coming up next
Please don't mad at my mansion or Rolex

Written by
Dwayne Lake

GET UP

Brothers and Sisters, get up out your seat
Find your passion or dream, and then move your feet
Nothing can come, sitting on your buns
Can't keep using excuses, about no funds
Be the captain, make it happen, make it work
Don't procrastinate like a stupid jerk
Stop being crazy lazy won't you get up
Drink and energy drink, pour coffee in your cup
Can't get nothing done laying in bed
Sit at the table make a plan use your head
Stop waiting for the mail, government hand out
Start your business show what you all about
Be the leader of the pack, don't follow behind
Dig deep in your brain the knowledge of your mind
Life is a struggle, hustle, bustle, plus grind
Reward comes when you cross the finish line

Written By
Dwayne Lake

LOVING YOU

Roses are reds, violets are blue
There's none more lovely than you
loving you is always easy
because the way you please me
you make me feel oh so real
I want none other you seal the deal
your all Ive could ever ask
Kepping you happy will be my task
You've been like a breath of fresh air
That why I care, share and will always be there
Your love it keeps me so excited
I'm so glad that we've finally united
Together as one never apart
You've stole the key to my heart
Loving you has me more motivated
I'm so happy this bond we've now created
Good thing I waited just to be with you
I feel that this love with you is true
let's keep this thing going never let it end
You more than my love, you're my bestfriend.

Written by
Dwayne Lake

I NEED YOU IN MY LIFE

I don't know why I deny you
every now and then I deify you
Lord you know i need you in my life

Not a year goes by, not a month goes by
Not a week goes by that I do not need you

Can you tell me why I resist you
now I realize that I miss you.
God you know I want you In my life

Not a day goes by, not a hour goes by
Not a minute goes by that I'm not thinking of you

Every time I close my eyes you were right there
In my heart and in my mind and you protect
me while I sleep Lord, Jesus, Thank you

Dwayne Lake

WHEN YOU RETURN

Chorus
I'll give any thing just to see your face
Thank you for your mercy—your love and your grace
Your son died upon the cross at Calvary
He sacrificed his life for a wretch just like me

Lead How can I thank you, repay you for all you've done
A father so good that he would give his only son
To put a price on the blessings bestowed upon me
I was so blind, but Lord you gave me the sight to see

I come to worship and praise your name
My love for you remains the same
I know some day you'll return to my life again.
Please forgive me for all of my sins

IS IT MY TIME

Is it my time to pray that your standing near
tell you I love you and I'll have no fear

Is it my time to turn my life to you confess
my sins and live a life that's true

Is it my time to sacrifice my all get back
on my feet every time I fall

Is it my time to stand before you King
You'll play back my deeds and will the angles sing

Is it my time to give up all the fun
Will he say he don't know me or son well done

Dwayne Lake

KEEP SEARCHING

I keep on searching, yearning just to see your face
I keep on searching for your mercy and your grace

I don't know how, I don't know when, I will come
to see your, face again, I'll keep waiting
I traveled mountains high and valley's low,
searching for the way that I must go
I'll keep searching

I know that you'll be coming back again, when will
the pain and suffering end, I'll keep waiting
Some nights I lay awake thinking of you, waiting
to hear a word from you, I'll keep searching

Wide is the gate, broad is the road that leads to you
Please cleanse my soul and make it pure

Dwayne Lake

GOD CREATED

My Jesus is over the ocean
My God he created the sea
My savors in charge of my life now
I'll wait till he come rescue me

My father is over the mountain
My Lord he created the trees
My maker controls my directions
What blessings bestowed upon me

He created us from the dirt on the ground
The most marvelous miracle I have found
My God made you and me, so we can praise and worship the
I will serve him for the rest of my life

He made me just like him in his image he
created me for the whole world to see
Jesus came into my life, and with his blood he sacrifice
I owe him the life that he wants me to live

My Jesus is over the valley's my God he created the hills my savor
made me in his image how good does his blessings they feel

Dwayne Lake

He's renewed in me a clean and fresh spirit he's enriched
and vitalized, touched my soul he has made me brand new,
and for him I will stay true will never backslide or turn
my life around Now that I'm shining like a pure and solid
gold this new meaning to my life shall not grow old
I'll stand bold and won't be shame, on the rock in Jesus name
I won't trade or forsake, the steps, that I, have made

My Lord he made the earth
To life that he gave birth
Our God poured out the rain
To wash away the pain

My Lord lit up the moon
I know he's coming soon
Illuminate the sun
He gave his only one

THEY'LL BE TIMES

They'll be some times when you will fall
And then some days you'll hit the wall.
Just put your trust and never doubt
That's what my God is all about

Mom said there'll be some days like this
Because your on the devils list
Stand to the word instilled in you
Then you will know just what to do

When life has got you down and out
And you just want to scream and shout
You feel the pains to much to bare
Call on the Lord for he'll be there

Feels like some bricks upon your back
Just then is when satan attack
Just know that you can play that game
Pray to the Lord don't be ashamed

Now this is what you have to do
Call on my God to your rescue you
Just stick and jab stay on your feet
That devils hold you can defeat

Dwayne Lake

Sometimes you feel that you can win
And then some days you can't pretend
Don't worry and now don't you fret
Cause all my needs the Lord has met

I can stand here and I'll testify
You'll never hear my Jesus lie.
Look Satan right between the eye
Now don't you move or don't you cry..

Don't stand there and you be afraid
Because your debt my Jesus paid
Just know that you are due your crown When
he return the trumpets sound

Lord don't take your loving arms of protection
away from me
I need you to be my love and affection
don't go away from me

WILL U RUN

Gangster, tough boy, thug what you going to do
When the Lord crack the sky and come back for you
Will you run, will you hide, boy won't you come inside
Get up off them streets and forget about your pride

This song is dedicated to hustlers on the street
Got this vision from my God as I was laying fast asleep
He said to speak about the fellas In the world today
You got to put a message out there bring them all my way

Talk about the hurt, the pain and the damage they done
While they out there on the street with their life on the run
Let them know that I can save them, with
the blood make them clean
All this work for me be done no matter how hard it seem

Lord put upon my mind give me the words to say
let me change this whole wide world and for this nation I pray
A traditional rendition not coming that way
Put his mission on my heart and with the knowledge convey

To the thugs, dealers, killers prostitutes and pimps
The muggers, robbers, thieves with the crime attempts
Here's my hand take the plan to the Lord I will lead
He can get you off them streets and supply your needs.

Dwayne Lake

You stand out on the street and flex your weight
You don't even give a care about the life you take
You living your life, like there's no end
Think the homies on the block is your family and your friend

But I want to show brother another road to take
Cause your life is based upon the decisions that you make
Come with me my brother get into the word
Cause Gods coming back so forget what you heard

Up and down our streets you trying to pump fear
Then you out there on the corner selling drugs and drinking beer
Pull the wool on our kids make them join your gangs
As time marches on you still doing your thing

But let me tell you my homie
it's time to get right Cause the Lord is
coming back like a thief in the night
So fall to your knees, cause we must confess
And ask the Lord to take us from our mess, and this stress

You crying heaven I need a hug an excuse of a thug
Trying to sweep the dirt you did under the rug
But God he got the tape and he gonna play it back
So you better get your life together and clean up your act

Dwayne Lake

When he put you on the stand you can't call upon your man
It's hot down there in hell you can't even use a fan
So think about that now while you doing all your deeds
When you running from the cops all night at them high speed

You a baller, shot caller think you are the man
But this life that you live, Is not Gods plan
You the man phat sedans with your chains and trucks
You spread that dope around and collect them bucks

Don't you know by now homeboy that's way of the world
You beat up on your homies and you pimp them girls
Check it out my brother that anit even the move
Why you taking, please stop faking, what you trying to prove.

To all my young homies and all my grown men
Some of yawl that I grew up with and pass by now and then
It's time to live right be a solder for the Lord
Did you know eternal life could be your reward

So why accept the devil that's a means to an end
Did you know that Jesus Christ died for all your sins
Now you might say homeboy what that really mean
It's a chance to get right tonight and come clean

Dwayne Lake

So come in to this house he will give you rest
He will get you off them streets and all that mess
just confess with thy mouth that he is Lord
lets get those other guys out there on one accord

Accept my God as your personal best
Give your life sacrifice you will pass that test
Straighten up make that change boy it won't be hard
Now your proud sing out loud give the glory to God

HEAR MY CRY

Lord I call you, on my knees
Won't you help me, help me please I've been running
way too long Won't you help me make it home

Oh my Lord won't you hear my humble cry

Lord I need you day to day
Please now bless me every way
I've been down and out just too much
Lord I need your loving touch

I've been leveled
To the ground
No greater love than you
I have not found

Hear my cry Wipe my eye live for you (my Lord) til I die
stay by me near my side Get on board father let me ride

Take me Lord to that place
I just want to see your face to that place you have
prepared with this faith in you I won't be scared

Dwayne Lake

Awesome Ruler

In this day and time we live in the world is full of sin
brothers are fighting brothers friends are killing friends
Our leaders they plot against a nation just like they play a game of chess
Dictating there orders to our country for me they feel what's best

We can't depend on this system for it has always let us down
Conformed to the rules of the U.S. It seems our hands are often
bound Were supporting all other places we that do have the plan
Instead of taking care of our home we rather go extend a hand

So often we put our trust in man never to really
understand the Lord is the means to our end
In him we can depend
Just put your faith in him believe
Don't worry you'll never be deceived
My God will never let you down
His love is forever found.

Nations are fighting nations just for a piece of land
Lord they don't really understand that the world is in your hands
We must turn to our savor in this day and time of war
Put our faith in the master until the lord he says no more

Dwayne Lake

He will heal our cities and he will cultivate our land
We must conform to his orders and we
should follow his righteous plan

God is awesome ruler
The Lord is the king of kings
He will fight your battles
My Lord will do all things.

He will never leave you Deceive you or let
you down Put your trust in Jesus
He'll always be around

Dwayne Lake

I WONDER

Sometimes I wonder am I down here all along
and will I ever someday make it home
Just to see your face your love and grace your truth
and your mercy, is all I need, for me you bleed

Wondering this time, am I doing your true will
or am I passing mountains chasing hills
I need to know—please won't you show—the road
that I must take to get to you—What must I do

We try to climb sometimes we know that we can fall
Thanks for the blood you shed for me you paid it all We
know we're only men and yet we all have sinned
A pleasing life for you Is the way that we can make it in

Sometimes I don't realize that you are here for me
At times I'm much too blind I can not see
Just to keep the faith, belief and trust
Stand strong and never bend, it's hard win, I can't pretend

Wondering this time have I, gave all that I can give
and helped that needed soul, so It can live
I know that I must sacrifice, for you I give my
life, I feel alone, please take me home

Dwayne Lake

Now a revelation has come upon my life to made me
see just exactly what your love it means to me

Now I can finally realize the joy and happiness inside
and I can sing and praise your holy name out loud

Lord we often wonder if we're following your plan
We've travel such a distance but we yet to understand at
time we are frustrated, but we're acting from our flesh
Please now Lord— won't you guild us thought the night

Dwayne Lake

Bring All Your Problems

I saw you setting, In the corner, all alone
I step to you asked what was wrong
You said that you were feeling lonely and sad
Cause just last night they made mad.

I have a friend, that you, can tell what's wrong
Don't need a pager or cell phone
Fall to your knees and he will hear your cry
He'll wipe the tear right from your eye

If your contemplating your problems and you don't
know what to do Bring your problems
to my father for his love for you is true
If your feeling sad and lonely and you feel that
no one care He will never turn love from
you for my God he'll be right there
If you used up all resources and you have nowhere to turn
If his favor you desire and his grace is what you yearn
Just you bring those issues before him lay your
drama down to rest He will give you all the
answers for my God knows what is best

Dwayne Lake

You gave up you could not continue to fight
You tried to battle with all your might
The race goes to the swift not the strong
You'll reach the finish before to long

Now don't give up my friend please don't give in
God's got the victory to win
He'll be there the Lord won't let you down
No longer lost you can be found

Oh He will never let you down (you down I'll always be found)
His love and grace how sweet the sound (his love
how sweet the sound) Just put your trust in him
you'll see (just put your trust you'll see)
And lean on the everlasting — mercy

See You say that you got issues don't know what to do
Let me take you to my father Where his promise is
true He would never forsake you or let you fall
When your backs against the wall he's the one to call
So now your down and out and your in despair
Then your feeling all depressed like nobody would care
To share

Dwayne Lake

PASS THE KNOWLEDGE

Pass the knowledge want you give it to a friend
Let us come together put that drama to a end
Yes we can do it if we just give it a try
I'll keep it real There's no reason for a lie
You share with me then I can share to you
Let's put our minds together there aint nothing we can do
See we can make it don't have to fake it
If you can dish it then I know that you can take it

Check It I'm on the grind I've got to shine
See I'm not blind man because I use my mind
Use intellect just to gain me more respect
I earn the funds so go head and sign my checks
I don't work hard I'm doing it smart
See my protection is a team of bodyguards
I bought a cook I got ten maids
Guess that's the benefit of making sure you paid
I'm trying to reach some say I preach
If I influence then I did my job to teach
Nobody schooled me on how to get that credit
If you don't have it well then you can just forget it
I had to learn to grow up and be a man
Look you not nothing unless you can own some land
It's who you know not even who you be
Not what you got It's about maturity.

Dwayne Lake

Now get your pencil write this on your pad
Do the research or believe you gone be had
It's not your fault that you didn't get taught
Awe you got taken for that junk you bought
So don't be bitter like them sour grapes
You'll know the next time just procrastinate
You might get burned roasted like some toast
I've learned my lessons I'm not even bout to boast
I'll testify on how the Lord he blessed
Don't need them club bars drinking all that mess
I've lived that life then that got played out
The lap of luxury is what I'm all about
Don't have to live from check to the next check
Now when you make it homie please protect yo neck
Cause see they coming to take all that you have
Now If you let them then set back watch them laugh.
I'll wrap this up before I close this message
Resist temptation is that really what the test is
Not rocket science just use some common sense
The confirmation see it leads to evidence
I'm going deep I hope you get the meaning
To catch the spirit give yo soul a thorough cleaning
You might be smart or even be street-wise
Use your brains you can open up some eyes
You seek relief under all that stress
You been through hell so now let me see yo best

Dwayne Lake

I know you wiser stronger and much better
Oh now you've realize got to get yo thing together
Well now you feel me believe in what I say
I know tomorrow just might bring a brighter day
So keep it tight stand on what you know
If this is yo time well then walk in through that door

DYSFUNCTIONAL

We love God but why we hate
Family retaliate
Money often is the root
Evils never really cute
Why you stab me in my back Look how at the way you act Get
yo hand up out my pocket Got to tie It down, pad lock it.
Tell me why we got to fight
Don't you know two wrongs not right
Brother why you mad at me
Can't you see we famity
We all try to get ahead
Before too long, we'll all be dead Don't you see our time is few
You do for me I'll do for you Sister don't you feel my love
Is money all that we think of
What's good for goose good for gander
Put me to shame then you slander
Why you drag me throuugh the dirt
Horrimie don't you know that hurt
Often times your tif for tat
You really got to be like that?
We like crabs off in a barrow This road we on is really narrow
We together need some space The truth around up In our face
We in this box but we can't speak Attention what
we really seek Whispering behind my back

Dwayne Lake

The Devil busy on attack
Often times we sell our soul
The Prince of darkness take control
Do unto me do it to other
My brother from another mother
Tell me why it's hard to share
Everybody out there
It seems nodody really care
This old world is really cold
Words that cut big & bold
Get over on me then you beat
Take advantage lie then cheat
Cut me down with yo tongue
You the Judge so now I'm hung
Treat me worse than a slave
Slash my my back I misbehave
Leave me on the table
We act like we Cain and Able
Put me in the Lions Den
Thought you said you was my friend
You told me wrong you lied to me
Is this bout some jealousy
Why we all cant get along
If I'm right I can't be wrong!

Dwayne Lake

TALK TO JESUS

If your ever feeling lonely, or your down and in despair
When it seems that no ones listening, not a friend to really care
Talk to Jesus he will hear you, he won't turn his back on you
His awesome love is always faithful everlasting and so true

Talk to Jesus He'll never let you down Talk to Jesus He'll
always be around Talk to Jesus In him you can depend
Talk to Jesus He's there from begging to end

May the words from my mouth, and the love from
my heart, be pleasing in your sight on my part
As I come to you and pray, give me righteous words
to say, Don't turn your love away, Oh my God.

Talk to Jesus, Talk to the Lord
Every battle fought, he'll be your shield and sword
Don't you worry, have faith don't doubt
When a problem rise the Lord can work it out

Dwayne Lake

THANK YOU LORD

If the Lord allowed your eyes to see another day,
You should bow your head to Heaven and then begin to pray
Thank the father for another chance to see the light
We take for granted that he could take us in the night
My father I come to you down here on my knees
Lord I need your blessings won't you help me please
Give me health and strength start me on my way
I worship, praise your name for another day
you watched over me as I slumber and sleep
Thank you for my life and my soul you keep
You have been oh so faithful so true to me
Broke the shackles off and you set me free
You let me spread my wings just like a dove
Watched me from clouds and you showed me love
Now check it Late one night as I start to fall
Lord your awesome name I had to call
You came to my rescue you were down for me
I was so blind you woke me up to see
You came and turned the darkness into bright light
Your love is like an eagle as it will take flight.

Thank you Lord you open up my eye
You wipe my tear when I had to cry
Embraced the ground when I had to fall
God you know you are my all and all You
had my back when they tried to take

Dwayne Lake

The hard earned money worked hard to make
That's why Lord I'm going to do your will
You made the robbers flee now I pay my bills
It's so hard out on these streets
Your word helps keep me on my feet
Your name keeps me from getting down
Cause I know someday you'll be around
I can call him anytime just to connect
And don't even have to write no check
I don't have call no physic line
Cause my father's going give me a piece of mind

Lord teach me the right words to say
Show me the way that I need to pray
Lord you have the key to unlock my heart
Please let my light shine you are my God
Show me how to live, live just like you
And do all the things that you would do
Father would you help me treat my neighbor right
To live in harmony and not to fight
God teach me to turn the other cheek
let them know it's not a sign of being weak
Lord show me how to hold my words
If you don't curse them out your not a nerd
Won't you clap your won't you stomp your feet
Help me praise the Lord to this reggae beat
Jamaican, apostolic Baptist, Christian
Give it up to my God for he has the plan

Dwayne Lake

Open up your bible don't be deceive
And won't you lift your hands if you do believe
let's worship honor, glorify his name
If you know my savior then you'll do the same
There so much about him that I can say
He open up the sea and he made a way
Fish and bread five thousand he feed Walk
upon the water to peter he said
Put his hands on the blind helped the man to see
Now think of the things he could do for we
You cry to the Lord that you need a fee
When Lord can change the course of history
We only call his name when we are in need
Our faith is just the size of a mustered seed We'd
been upon the cross and we would wine
Thank you father that you put this message on my mind

GOD IS GOOD

If he woke you up this morning let you see another day
Got you up out of your bed and start you on your way
Just get up out your seat and wave ya hands
Give praise unto to the Lord Like David Dance, Dance Dance

If God's been good to you then get up and clap your hands
Move your body to this beat and do this holy dance
If you see another day why do you parlay
Like you guaranteed some time won't you start to repay

His love is like a river and the flow never ends
So pray unto the Lord on your knees they must bend
God has help me through my trials and tribulation
Brought me out of darkness revealed a revelation

To me he helped me see and to be I need to be
In his plan a better man on his land a true Christian
Distractions and diversions have got you down
Recognize that his blessing is the greasiest I've found

Temptations and the traumas come along your way
And the pressures of this life they disrupt your day
He's been better to me than my life long friends
With his love and his blood he washed away all my sin

Dwayne Lake

Now put your faith in the master lay burdens to rest
Better hurry trust don't worry so you'll pass the test
Till the end so tell a friend about the works he's done
He sacrifice his family and he sent us his son

He helped you with your payments when the bills where due
And he start to heal your body when you had the flu
late up in the night when your back on the wall
If he ever picked you up when you started to fall

You looked unto the word when you needed advice
More than radical I'm gone get ridiculous for Christ
Been a doctor, and a lawyer, been savor to me
Made it rain forty days he even parted the sea

Well the time is now and the day is today
To accept the Lord accordingly then walk in his way
He can come back in the day or like a thief in the night
To the people of the world hey yo It's time to get right

God is good and God he is so Great
His mercy love and grace I appreciate
So accept him now and don't procrastinate
Cause when the Lord return don't think he gone wait

Dwayne Lake

He has so many blessings that you can't receive
He can bring you out your issues if you truly believe
In him without a doubt you just keep the faith
The desires of your heart he might make you wait

To the end so tell a friend to request the Lord
Then present the enemy with your shield and sword
Cause when you do battle get back up in the saddle
He'll try to knock you off you block pull your chain or rattle
like a snake he like to sneak have his way and make you weak
Try to get you from behind and try to steal your mind
Stay focus on my God with your faith it won't be hard
Cause the enemy make a fool of you, but God will make you smart

Lord I testify for me you been good
You have kept your eye on me protect me in the hood
When I talk about your blessings the things that've done
I get the joy plus much to see the devil run

He know I got him beat when I stand my ground
Toe to toe blow for blow I beat them demons down
I love to praise my God caause he's worth the wait
The blessings from on high I anticipate

Dwayne Lake

His return oh how I yearn I concerned plus discern
To make it where he dwells is my main concern
To live that life that he wants me to live
And to give all of me that I need to give

To him rededicate and to him we demonstrate
The presence of the Lord is here we can't wait
So go and tell somebody that he will return let them
always seek his face cause they need to learn

Dwayne Lake

LORD I HAVE A QUESTION

Chorus Lord I have some questions that's been on my mind
I don't want to be the one of many left behind
Can you tell me all the things on earth I need to do
You'll give it me straight to the point and true
Lord I want know, am I doing your will?
No I saw you in the store and you were trying to steal
God I need to know am I working your plan?
You won't open up the Bible and obey commands
Father have I live the life that you want me to live?
No you always stuff your pockets and not to give
Savor do I treat my neighbors and my family right?
When you come outsidethey have to hide you ready to fight
All the blessings that you have, can I please have some?
Every since you were a child you've cursed your mom
Is it pleasing my behavior or the way I act?
When you often get offended, then you on attack
Have I told the world about you, brought them close to you
You manipulate and perpetrate to do what you do
Have I gave the ten percent of the pay I earn
You spend your money on the women like you got to burn

Dwayne Lake

Do I confess with my mouth that Christ is Lord?
You've tried to claim your name to fame, so that's yo reward
Can I count on being saved just by calling your name
You have tried to get to fortunes with them gambling games
Am I eager too impatient too discourage to wait
You have shown me no trust where is all your faith
Have I stood and testify, told of works you've done
No you told a test a lie and then when problems you run
Do I fast and meditate on you the way I should
I saw you hanging and gang banging in your Englewood hood.
By the power of the enemy I accept defeat
I guess you do cause through your life you continued to cheat
Do I let my light shine take it wherever I go
Your often deep into your flesh then you out for show
Have I opened up the door, hear your voice, to knock
I relay this message to you, but you checking your clock.
Lord I never harmed a soul or a person I've hurt
You won't even sacrifice or give a homeless a shirt
I've never took money not a person I've robbed
But it was hard for you to even get your brother a job
I would never bare a witness put no one before you
You put your woman on a pedestal so that's not true
I would never disrespect you use your name in vain
But you often slap your sister that too a shame
I have tried to turn my life around and give to you
Then you out there on the town telling lies not true

Dwayne Lake

God I did my best to love you tried to be your best son
But you walk around the city tooting drugs and guns
Lord I never have forsake you shame your name blaspheme
But you would Often get unraveled then come loose at seems
When you come back here to get me with you I'll dwell?
I know the path that you are taking is the road to hell

IF YOU WERE TO DIE TONIGHTE

If you were to die tonight, would it be well with your soul
Will the Lord turn his back or leave you out in the cold
Would he say my faithful servant that's a job well done
Or depart from me, I know you not, you had too much fun

Check it out now
As it is written there is none righteous none
Not the preacher, not the rabbi, not the priest, but it's the son
Of man, for all have sinned and come short of Gods glory
Every deed that you have done for every time you told that story
For the wages of your sins, is death sayeth the Lord
The gift of God, through Jesus Christ, eternal life reward
Compensation from your job is a paycheck that you earn,
But the wages of your sin is only death so please don't burn.
Though we never saw his face in his works we put our trust
It's time we get our lives together cause now that is a must.
Whomsoever call upon the Lord they shall be saved
He can take you by earthquake, hurricane or title wave
All the times you played the fool then thought it was all
fine He's not coming back by water but by fire the next
time So repent with yo mouth cause we must confess
He won't take no lie, no alibi, or nothing less.

Dwayne Lake

See now
Death is eternal in a place called hell
So make your life successful in the Lord don't fell
Cause I am told that hells a place that is hotter than hot
Some people think vacation spot that's something it's not

* Would you really like to roam a home of all brimstone
Don't you think about a calling card, you can't call home
But to dwell with him eternally he has prepared
Live your life out to his will then you will be spared
Don't you lie, steal, kill, or cheat don't fornicate
These are some of his commandments, so now what's the wait
Believe in your heart that Jesus rose from the dead
* Plant it deep into your soul and then embed into yo head
Jesus lived a sinless life then he died on the cross
He sacrificed and shed his blood so we won't be lost
So now get your house in order be ye saved and sanctified
Seek ye first the kingdom of God and you will not to hide

I'm coming to my people, bold live and direct
Asking Gods blood covering protect yo neck
Cause this Chi-town that we live is often based on race
Pray to the Lord he'll shield you put the hate in its place

Dwayne Lake

God here is my weakness on my life's stronghold
Satan's playing with my mind and he's controlling my soul
By the power of your spirit please Lord set us free
I surrender all enticement draw me now unto the

He won't put no more upon you than your able to bare
Jesus save me from myself then deliver my prayer
If we hold on to the truth plus stay true to the faith
If we stand the test of time with our patients we wait cause now
* When the battles is over we shall wear a crown
We will hear the angels sing then see the saints all march around
We will bask in paradise over gold we all will roam
Swing low sweet chariot coming to take me home

Dwayne Lake

GORLY TO GOD

In all the things you do give the glory to God let
him know you appreciate dedicate your heart
Magnify and acknowledge for the blessings bestowed
For the love, mercy, grace and the favors he showed

Give recognition to God whom the credit is due
For the pain and suffering he's brought you through
As the praises go up then blessing come down
I love to raise his holy name from mountains abound
People come to hear the word of God from miles around
They seem to feel the happiness and love I've found
Cause this joy that he bless me with is truly my own
I still away and meditate at work or home
I am on the battle field lighting for my Lord
And I came prepared to fight with my Bible the sword
I love to praise and worship while I'm singing his song
When I'm down and depressed and I'm feeling alone
Because he that believed give the glory to God Make
sure the savior's deep down into your heart
Cause to deal with this world you need him in your life
To gain desires of your life means sacrifice

If you got concerns or you feeling some doubts
let me tell you what this ministry all about
Not a chance to perpetrate or gain some clout

Dwayne Lake

But to tell you how God has brought me out
Got to glorify the Lord, cause it's not about me
He took the shackles off my spirit and set me free
He put the fire way deep down into my soul
Emotions that my mind and body can't control.
In all the things you do just acknowledge his name
To save and give life was the reason he came
He'll give a chance to choose of your own free will
But don't forget that time your body he healed
You forgot when he kept your butt from that jail
He can even keep your soul from the depths of hell
All the reasons that I give my all and all to God
He's taken out bitterness and soften my heart

Why they only call your name when they on sick bed
Or when they in that Institute stressed in the head
Why they only find religion when they in state pens
They don't think about that crime when they commit that sin
They love to call your name when they on death row
When it's time to pull that switch it a media show
And tell of how you fail as you lay in that cell
With no way of bail, you prepare for hell
took prayer out the schools then they brought guns in
They turned there back my God then the killings begin
Let's turn this world around put God in the plan

Dwayne Lake

He got this whole wide world in the palm of hand
The nation put a man in charge he shoulders the weight
The Lord is higher than the highest head of states
I'm walking with my father that set us free
In all the things you do give the glory to he.